D1290741

*"Charette strikes me as a strong character ;
I discern uncommon energy, rare audacity in his
actions ; he displays the mark of genius."*

Napoleon.

It is ten in the morning on this 3rd Germinal in Year IV. Or at least so says the Republican Calendar, little used in the fervently Catholic Vendée, where people persist in recalling that this 23rd March 1796 is also the Wednesday of Holy Week. Somewhere between Les Lucs and La Chabotterie, shots ring out from a spinney, La Tremblaye. Ten grenadiers

# THE WAR OF THE VENDÉE ENDS AT LA CHABOTTERIE

from the Vosges and Paris Brigade train their fire on an already lifeless corpse. "It's Charette !" And so it would seem, judging by the hat decorated with the famous white panache now lying in the mud.

## "Give me your hat and save yourself !"

"At last !" exults Brigadier Valentin, who believes that three long years of civil war have thus been ended. For it was in March 1793 that the Vendée, a region of which until then few had heard, rose in revolt against the Republic. An area equivalent in size to a single departmental region, pitted against the ninety-two other departmental regions : an act of madness. Yet these peasant folk, formerly the object of so much scorn, won some resounding victories. The soldiers of the Mainz battalions, the best republican troops

*The final struggle.*

available, were sent to fight them. And one hundred thousand Vendéens, fleeing their burning villages, crossed the Loire only to be slaughtered in Le Mans, Savenay or Nantes ...

*On the way to be execute*

Francois Athanase Charète, Général En Chef de l'Armée Royale, Et Catholique de la Vendée. fusillé à Nantes Placé des Agriculteurs le 9 germinal l'an 4

Noirmoutier

Fonteclose

Le

Ile d'Yeu

Les Lucs-
-sur-Boulogne

Forêt de Grasla

La Jaunaie

lleville

la Chabotterie

F. LAURENT

The Republican Convention then set out to obliterate all traces of this accursed territory. On a Vendée drained of its lifeblood, General Turreau unleashed his infernal columns, with orders to destroy or exterminate everything in their path. But in a last-ditch effort most of the few remaining able-bodied men rallied instinctively round a general who had until then lain in the shadow of leaders such as Cathelineau, Lescure, d'Elbée, Bonchamps or La Rochejaquelein. And it is this man, the elusive Charette, the scourge of so many republican columns sent in his pursuit, who now lies dead.

But can they be sure ? The corpse is examined more closely. To everyone's astonishment, the dead man is not Charette ! The body is that of Pfeiffer, a former deserter who, seeing Charette about to be captured, took his general's hat and laid down his own life to give Charette one final chance to escape.

*A stained-glass window at Le Pin-en-Mauges shows Charette accompanied to his execution by a priest who has sworn allegiance to the Republic, but receiving, at his sister's instigation, absolution from a non-juring priest stationed at a window.*

### "While a single wheel remains, Charette's cart* will rumble on"

Some rifle shots away, in the village of La Boulaye, Charette regains his breath. This thirty-eight-year-old man, whom the previous year the King of France had called the second founder of the monarchy, has been no more than a hunted animal for the past three months. With Robespierre's demise, on 28th July 1794, the Reign of Terror ceased to foment the rebellion. On the same day, the newly-founded Republic released from prison one of the many such young republican generals of the time, giving him the task of pacifying the Vendée. Lazare Hoche put an immediate end to the persecution of the clergy and the slaughter of the peasant population, and the Vendée's inhabitants are now attempting to forget the horrors of war and rebuild their lives. Certainly, Charette can still count on the local population's silent collusion, but even most of his officers have laid down their arms. The mainspring of the insurrection is now broken. "While a single wheel remains, Charette's cart will rumble on", declared Charette, ever steadfast in his resolve, though now able to count on the support of thirty followers at most.

Since dawn, he has already had to escape capture by the two-hundred-strong 4th Hérault Battalion, then the one hundred and fifty grenadiers of the Vosges and Paris Brigade. Eighty soldiers of the "Avenger" battalion now appear before him, and Charette seeks cover in the thickets of a small nearby wood, known to the local peasantry as the communal wood, since they are accustomed to plundering its resources right under the very nose of the Lord of La Chabotterie. It is here that Charette has a date with his destiny.

### "To you alone did I wish to surrender"

His destiny assumes the form of twenty-six-year-old Jean-Pierre Travot, who leads a troop of three hundred and fifty mounted chasseurs. Charette is completely surrounded and knows that all is probably lost. Even so, he believes that there may yet be a means of escape. But his route is barred by Captain Vergez, who wounds him in the head and right shoulder.

With blood clouding his vision, Charette is still trying to flee when, exhausted, he collapses into unconsciousness. His servant, the faithful Bossard, who carries him on his back, is soon struck down dead. Chevalier de Lespinay, who tries to hide him, is also killed.

---

*the French word "charrette" means "cart", hence the play on words.*

*The entrance to La Chabotterie.*

*The Chabots' coat of arms : three golden chabots face on, two and one (the chabot is a large-headed variety of angler-fish).*

Dealing many a sabre blow, Vergez disarms the Vendéen General, gashing his wrist and cutting off three of his fingers.

- Is it really him ? inquires Travot.
- Yes, by Charette's word of honour !
- Long live the Republic, long live Travot ! cry the soldiers.
- Would you be Travot ?
- Yes, I am.
- None too soon, to you alone did I wish to surrender.

It is half past twelve. The defeated general is taken away and held in the Château de la Chabotterie's kitchens, a vast room with an enormous granite fireplace.

Four hours later, under heavy escort, Charette leaves La Chabotterie on a journey leading him to Nantes, the place of his execution. The War of the Vendée ends at La Chabotterie.

## A residence in its twin setting

Having retraced the astounding story of an obscure midshipman who later comes to rule the Vendée, we will discover together the places where his memory continues to live on. But beforehand, let us take the time to visit La Chabotterie. It is here that, in order to evoke the dramatic history of the Vendée in its proper context, the Departmental Regional Council has sought to recreate the surrounding bocage environment, without which it is not possible to understand either the communities which inhabit this area or their singular approach to fighting a war. Let us begin with the residence itself : a granite jewel set within its gardens. Visitors should not expect to see the luxuriousness and mock pastoral settings so fashionable at Versailles. But those receptive to charm and authenticity will be won over by its XVIIIth century graces.

*An old photograph, taken from the gardens.*

### Five centuries of history

At the end of the Hundred Years' War, the Lower Poitou Region is rebuilding from the ruins. In this XVth century, in a small, marshy valley traversed by a stream, the Isoire, the Chabot family had built the Château which has since borne their name. In actual fact, at this time La Chabotterie probably only comprises a simple two-storey edifice, with a enclosed courtyard in front : this structure is the present-day main building, whose frame still shows where the openings were located.

## LA CHABOTTERIE, OR THE ART OF LIVING IN A VENDÉE MANOR-HOUSE

The Château subsequently undergoes much alteration, especially in the XVIIth century. While the region increasingly specializes in livestock farming and becomes a bocage criss-crossed with hedges, two wings are added to the Château's main building.

The following century is at once beneficent and tragic. Who would have thought that the art of gracious living, illustrated most eloquently by the Château's gardens, would be brutally interrupted by a dreadful civil war ? And yet as the scene of Charette's capture, the Château owes its fame to this very drama.

In the XIXth century, not unlike the Vendée as a whole, which seeks refuge behind its clergy and nobility, La Chabotterie is further embellished by a chapel and tower.

Most recently, Vendée Departmental Regional Council has set out to make this place of remembrance a point of access for those who wish to understand Vendéen history.

Following the further devastation caused by the Wars of Religion in the XVIth century, lordly families such as the Chabots are the architects of the region's agrarian landscape as it has remained almost to our own day. Exercising their feudal right of redemption, which offers them first refusal on land put up for sale, these nobles join plots of land together to create larger tenant farms covering thirty to forty hectares. These *métairies* specialize in livestock farming, especially in beef cattle, which are first used to pull ploughs and then fattened up for the Paris market.

## TENANT FARMERS, BEEF CATTLE AND BOCAGE

### The bocage is created

This explains why the tenant farmers gradually create the bocage, a grid network of hedges which are primarily intended to prevent livestock grazing on a neighbour's land. But the bocage also facilitates land drainage, as at La Chabotterie, where small water-meadows lay at right angles to the course of the Isoire. And in this region lacking woodland, the hedges were planted with trees polled to the height of a man : the characteristic outline of the pollards, whose branches were cut down periodically for firewood. In periods of drought, which often scorch this pastureland, their leaves provided fodder for cattle.

*Gathering the hay.*

*La Chabotterie in its bocage setting.*

## SHOULD THE BOCAGE BE RESTORED ?

*Being concerned to make optimum use of ever larger items of machinery, and disinclined to waste their time maintaining hedgerows, farmers in the Vendée have pulled up some eight thousand kilometres of hedges, or eight million trees, in the past forty years or so. As a result, it is probable that the already chronic drought conditions in this region have been worsened still further. And it certainly true to say that, if this process of destruction is continued, the bocage will become an ill-defined, uninteresting and featureless plain.*
*This course of action may appear paradoxical at a time when, more than ever before, such emphasis is placed on the importance of a strong local identity, in attracting not only tourists of course, but also companies and personnel increasingly attached to their living environment.*

*Will the grants allocated by the Departmental Regional Council for replanting hedgerows be sufficient to restore our bocage ?*
*Should this not be everyone's concern ?*

## Close-knit local communities

In addition to the income derived from beef cattle, relative prosperity is ensured by the area's craft cloth-makers, who sell their goods both locally and to the American market. Few are poor, and even less rich, among the inhabitants of the bocage's villages and hamlets, whether craftsmen, tenant farmers or smallholders. The locals are all the happier to see one another, whether at mass or at evening gatherings, where all can enjoy the company of friends and neighbours, far from the abstract discussions which excite city folk. Admittedly, the local population would not be averse for all that to the changes proposed by the Revolution, but when the Republic seeks to deprive these people of their local parish priests and to deck them out in soldiers' uniforms, even scythes and pitchforks will become weapons of war. And the bocage will then form the maze in which the republican troops lose their way, fired on by peasant folk who, thanks to their regular poaching trips on the lands of their lords and masters, are pretty good shots.

*The Moulin de la Merlatière mill, as shown by the charter keeper of Le Landreau.*

Not wealthy enough, more often than not, for life at Versailles, the members of the local nobility serve in the armed services of the King, preferably in the Navy, and then return to their modest country

# THE MANOR-HOUSE IN THE XVIIth AND XVIIIth CENTURIES

seats, where they while away the time in endless hunting expeditions.

# A throwback to the Middle Ages

The tower which accommodates the stairway dates from 1611. This tower is made entirely of dressed stone, with a semi-circular doorway surmounted by an arc-shaped pediment. A bartizan projects from the south-west corner. This pretence at defensive arrangements probably reflects a certain way of thinking of the time ; just as proud boasts are made about a family's ancestry, the architecture incorporates a throwback to the Middle Ages.

The stairway gives access to a vast square pavilion, added to the northern aspect of the manor-house. This same period also sees the construction of the wings flanking the main courtyard. The farm which supplies produce to the lord of the manor has its own buildings, forming an extension to these wings.

*The semi-circular entrance, surmounted by an arc-shaped pediment and a shield bearing the arms of an illegitimate child of Bourbon lineage born to a Miss Chabot.*

## A blend of refinement and rusticity

In the following century, whereas many local nobles prefer to set up house in the towns, here the lord of the manor remains true to his lands. The present efforts to restore the manor-house seek to recreate the atmosphere of the XVIIIth century using solely period furnishings, in an attempt to evoke this highly particular blend of rusticity and refinement.

Furthermore, the exhibition of working models located in the south wing's attic allows visitors to set La Chabotterie in the context of an historical heritage as rich as it is unrecognized : that of the Vendée's manor-houses.

Set between the manor-house and the surrounding countryside lie the house's gardens : an exceptional setting linking culture and nature. In fact, almost everything has had to be recreated using the information provided by the Napoleonic cadastral survey and the few surviving physical details, so that classical gardens in the XVIIIth century style could be brought back to life.

# THE GARDENS, OR THE ART OF LIVING IN THE XVIIIth CENTURY

## An ordered world

These gardens surrounded by walls mark the continuation of the rigorously mathematical approach evidenced in the house's façade. Admittedly, allowance is made for the limited space available, there being no room for ornamental lakes or complex patterns of plants and flowers as at Versailles, yet the desire for an ordered world is nonetheless strongly felt. A strict symmetry of boxwood borders unfolds beneath the house's windows, the framework for carpets of flowers or mineral ornamentations. As the ground falls away, the geometrical pattern of the vegetable garden unfurls, joined up on one side by a porticoed rose garden and on the other by a line of topiaries.

## All nature is a garden

Yet how is it possible both to be sheltered from the outside world and not to feel stifled by so much rigour and economy of space ? The highly original solution comes from England : aha ! is the cry on coming upon the side opposite the house, which is only enclosed by a ditch and offers a view running the length of a magnificent bridle-path. This path, just like the orchard and the bocage, whether preserved or restored, gives the impression that, though reason might loosen its grip, all nature is a garden.

After the war, after the deliberate, gratuitous slaughter of its population, the Vendée becomes a land apart. Yet there is no hatred, just the fear of recalling so much horror. Religion, which represented the battle standard of the insurrection, will only continue to gain strength throughout the XIXth century. The Vendée offers its martyrdom up to God.

# "THE VENDÉE, ITS LIPS SEALED BY THE SIGN OF THE CROSS" *(Jean Yole)*

## The manor, the presbytery and the tenant farmers

In what is reputed to be a loyal region, the XIXth century also marks a return in strength by the nobility, which builds châteaux all over the Vendée. At La Chabotterie, saved from destruction because it was used as a republican headquarters, the house's interior is completely transformed. And a round tower is even added in the gothic style of the time. In the same process of reconstruction as in

*An idyllic scene at the Château du Bois Corbeau, as depicted by Baron de Wismes.*

the XVIth century, the old tenant farming system, having long since fallen into disuse, is re-introduced everywhere. The attitude shown by the local populations towards "our mast'r", as he is called, is now a curious blend of respect, familiarity and dissimulation.

With the advent of a Republic which adopts anticlericalism as its battle cry, the Vendée retreats still further behind its clergy and nobility. A chapel is built at La Chabotterie in 1883 : a holy alliance between the manor, the presbytery and the tenant farmers ...

## Charette and the Virgin in the Oak

Can it really be a coincidence ? In 1911, two monuments set just a hundred metres apart are unveiled. In a moving testimony to popular piety, a small shrine is built in the hollow of a enormous oak-tree reputed to be a thousand years old, to hold a statue of the Virgin Mary. In the same year, a cross decorated with fleurs-de-lis is erected in honour of Charette, on the very site where he was captured.

# La Chabotterie today : a place of remembrance

## Evocations of the War of the Vendée

As well as recreating the manor-house and its atmosphere in the XVIIIth century, Vendée Departmental Regional Council has set out to provide a variety of attractive, objective and lively educational approaches for those who wish to learn more about the War of the Vendée. Visitors will find a vast fresco in strip-cartoon form, an audio-visual presentation, a large temporary exhibition and the most advanced scenographic techniques.

## The heritage courses

Likewise, a programme of heritage courses is intended as an active, practical and stimulating educative framework for teachers, pupils and tourist guides. La Chabotterie hosts seminars offering an introduction to Vendéen history, and can serve as a starting point for the discovery of the Vendée's historical heritage.

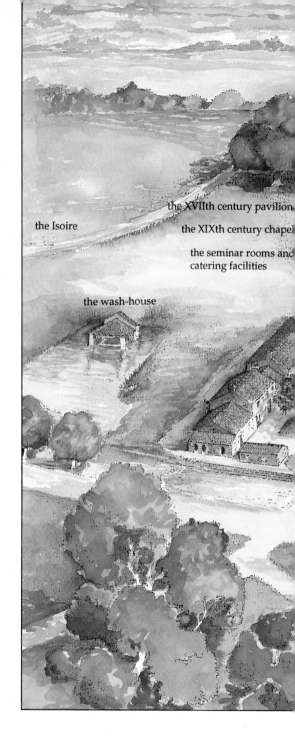

the Isoire

the XVIIth century pavilion

the XIXth century chapel

the seminar rooms and catering facilities

the wash-house

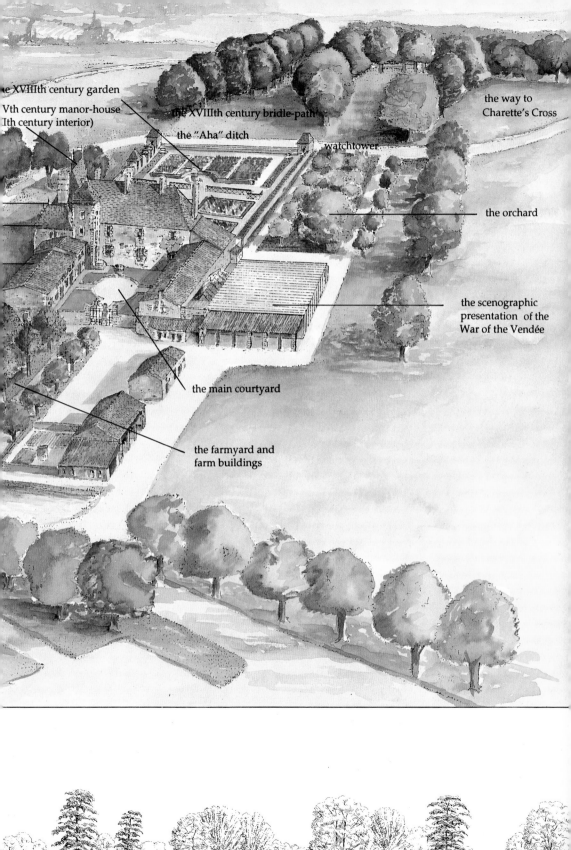

the XVIIIth century garden

Vth century manor-house
Ith century interior)

the XVIIIth century bridle-path

the "Aha" ditch

watchtower

the way to
Charette's Cross

the orchard

the scenographic
presentation of the
War of the Vendée

the main courtyard

the farmyard and
farm buildings

# CHARETTE

La Garnache, 14th March 1793. A small group hurries on its way to Fonteclose, a local manor-house. This band of peasant folk and craftsmen is barely recognizable : with a brisk step and a high tone, they are brandishing clubs, pitchforks and hunting rifles. The reason is that blood has flowed three days previously, at Machecoul. Enraged by the provocations of bourgeois profiting from the revolution, this perpetually submissive underclass has risen in revolt. But let there be no mistake : in seeking out Charette, they are not looking for a lord and master to re-establish an old régime which none lament in the slightest. They need someone to lead them in battle, against the repression which they know to be imminent. Leadership is the traditional role of the nobility : if this noble does not want to go along, they will compel him to do so.

## CHARETTE HIDES UNDER A BED

## They promised liberty, equality and fraternity

Rallying to the sound of the tocsin, locals from the surrounding districts invade the streets of Machecoul on the morning of 11th March. "Down with the militia !" is the cry addressed to the district administrators. The discontent is deep-rooted. The supporters of the new régime promised liberty, equality and fraternity. In fact, they were seen to claim all political responsibilities for themselves, fight over ecclesiastical property, increase taxes and persecute the clergy. Those who had done away with the hated militia now want to force the local lads to go far away to defend their revolution. "Let them go first !".

## All rebels shall be put to death

*A republican version of "snakes and ladders" (details).*

Utter incomprehension reigns between the demonstrators and the national guards who are now marching boldly against them. Why, wonder these bourgeois revolutionaries, do the very people whose happiness is their only wish here have the countenance of these uneducated, brutish and primitive peasants ? Too late ! Engulfed and their safety threatened, they fire on the demonstrators. The crowd surges forward and slaughters twenty or more guards. In the following days, similar disorders stir up the entire region. Unavailingly, the insurgents invoke the newly established, inalienable right to rebel against oppression ; unavailingly, they attempt to negotiate a settlement. On 19th March, the Convention decides that all rebels shall be put to death. The War of the Vendée has begun.

*The massacre at Machecoul whipped up republican imaginations and motivated the most terrible excesses.*

## The dark legend

The story goes that, rather than become the leader of a rebellion which he knows to be doomed, Charette hides under a bed. Yet he is forced to give way before the determination of these peasant folk. "Be certain to obey me," he is supposed to have threatened, "or your punishment shall be most severe".

*Charette leaving Fonteclose, as seen by Tom Drake.*

Yet at Machecoul, his involvement comes late in the day : those who had only recently flirted with the new régime have already formed a committee, chaired by a certain Souchu. On 23rd March, commanded by the aged Marquis de La Roche Saint-André, the rebels invest Pornic, a town loyal to the Republic, emptying the burgesses' wine cellars. When the latter return, they have no difficulty in slaughtering two hundred peasant soldiers sleeping it off. Even their three hundred prisoners are executed.

Souchu then has fifty republican prisoners held at Machecoul put to death. Such reprisals against fifty unarmed men contrast sharply with the astonishing leniency generally displayed by the Vendéens. This episode will nonetheless substantiate the dark legend of five hundred and fifty-two victims tortured to death by fanatical peasant folk. A story made up by Boullemer ... a one-time associate of Souchu.

It is only in retaking Pornic, on 27th March, that Charette gives the rebels of the Pays de Retz area their first victory and begins to assert his authority. Previously, this figure deemed weak and effeminate had been an object of much derision ...

*Pornic, as depicted by Tom Drake.*

24

> *""Remember that I am an officer in the French Navy and that honour is my only reward."*

Charette in 1786,
to an American captain who wished to bribe him.

## "STILL SLEEPERS CAN BE FEARSOME UPON WAKING" (NAPOLEON)

There is nothing to prefigure a grand destiny for little François-Athanase Charette de la Contrie, born on 21st April 1763, at Couffé near Ancenis, into a family possessing more noble lineage than material wealth. Fortunately for this son of a modest captain of infantry, his uncle and godfather, Charette de la Gascherie, a counsellor at the High Court in Rennes, pays for him to study with the Oratorians in Angers. Finding his way in the world is another matter altogether. Like many from the Lower Poitou Region, he cannot hope for promotion in a King's Army where companies and regiments have to be paid for. He therefore makes his career in the Navy.

*The "Hercule", the vessel aboard which, in 1782-1783, Charette took part in the American War. (Drawings of the stern ornaments and mouldings by Caffièri).*

## A very ordinary member of the gentry

Charette is made a midshipman on 20th March 1779, a sub-lieutenant in 1781 and a lieutenant in 1787. Eleven campaigns in all, including six in wartime. One anecdote which reveals his way of thinking is set during the American War : "Remember that I am an officer in the French Navy and that honour is my only reward," is his reply to an American smuggler who wished to bribe him.

Aside from that, all accounts agree with the opinion of his friend Las Cases, with whom he shares bed and board : Charette holds no promise whatsoever. "We were all of the judgement," Napoleon's famous secretary later explains to his Emperor, "that Charette was a rather common man of little distinction, cantankerous by nature and above all thoroughly indolent." At which the Emperor remarked : "Let there be no mistake : still sleepers can be fearsome upon waking".

## Asking for the daughter's hand, he marries the mother

The Revolution places Charette, and France's entire nobility, before a particularly painful dilemma. Should he follow those who, unwilling to jeopardize their careers, continue to serve the State ? In the Vendée, it should be remembered, the republican armies will be commanded by a Count (Canclaux), a Duke (Biron) and a Baron (Turreau de Linières). Charette, for his part, has little liking for the new attitudes agitating the crews. In 1790, he resigns his commission and, thinking about settling down, sets his sights on the daughter of a cousin. But the mother, fourteen years his senior, gives him to understand that she herself wishes to re-marry. She is a good match and owns, among other properties, the manor-house of Fonteclose. Our adventurer drops anchor.

*From the Port of Havana ...*

*... to the Port of Nantes.*

## An XVIIIth century embodiment of minor nobility

At this time, émigrés send members of the nobility hesitating to go into exile ironic reminders in the form of distaffs, a traditional symbol of womanhood. Charette therefore leaves for Koblenz, where the stilted atmosphere soon wearies him. He is then to be found at the Tuileries, in time to defend the King against the *sans culotte* revolutionaries, on 10th August 1792.

Having survived the slaughter, Charette only manages to escape imprisonment in Poitou by pointing to his friendship with General Dumouriez. Even if he is one of the future Vendéen leaders to have given the fewest assurances to the new régime, he tries, as do they all, to make himself inconspicuous.

Who at this time would recognize, in this XVIIIth century embodiment of minor nobility and delicate voluptuary interested in fine clothes and amorous adventures, the military leader who is to unnerve the Republic ?

Between March and June 1793, the Grand Royalist and Catholic Army wins a string of victories, taking in succession Thouars, Parthenay, Fontenay, Saumur and Angers. Nothing, it would appear, can stem this tide of Vendéen peasantry inexorably sweeping aside all republican troops in their path. Near the coast however, in Charette's area, matters do not follow the same course : the capture of Pornic on 27th March fails to make his authority complete.

# CHARETTE AND HIS BLACK SHEEP

## Troops dance to the sound of violins and musettes on the morning of the battle

On 13th April, Charette is beaten at Challans. Worse still, on the 22nd, considering his recruits to be deficient, he abandons Machecoul to Beysser. A reputation for cowardice goes before him as he withdraws to join Royrand, the officer commanding the centre, who gives him a cool reception. On the 30th at Legé, seeing his troops scattering once again, he has to rush forward to rally them. On 1st May, his own men call him a Judas. They fail to understand one whom the most serious reverses will never demoralize : he kills some mutineers himself, holds forth at then pardons the others, and in demanding their future obedience is hailed by his troops.

At last, on 17th May, he wins a victory near Lac de Grand-Lieu, and regains Royrand's respect by the same token. On 10th June, he retakes Machecoul ; beforehand, his troops had danced to the sound of violins and musettes into the early hours.

### A bevy of beautiful women

Hardened drinkers, inveterate pillagers who are sometimes cruel and always undisciplined, Charette's *Paydretz*\*, his famous *black sheep*, bear little resemblance to Cathelineau's pious band of followers. Neither do their commanders, such as Joly, a former surgeon, who dislikes the clergy and detests the nobility, or Guérin, Pageot, La Cathelinière et al, who are more like tribal chiefs jealous of their independence.

Nor does Charette resemble the other Vendéen generals. At his *Court* at Legé, according to one of his officers, "we were entertained as guests at a wedding". A bevy of beautiful women, his famous "Amazons", hovers around the General. "He took a different woman every night", asserts Michelet, guilty of exaggeration. One detail is certain though : despite having no ear for music, Charette never misses a dance. In complete contrast to the mortifications of General Lescure, the Saint of Poitou, who wears a hair shirt. All have one point in common, however : they all know that they are going to die.

*A municipal officer wearing his sash.*

\* *inhabitants of the Pays de Retz area.*

*Vendéen peasant soldiers. (Detail from the painting "Death of General Moulin, Battle of Cholet, 1793", by Jules Benoit-Lévy).*

## Charette the unloved ?

We can now understand why this man of pleasures is so frowned upon by the Grand Army, which calls him *the little naval cadet*. Neither do the Pays des Mauges peasant folk understand their counterparts from the Pays de Retz, who are less devout but even more democratically minded than they are. Yet one reason why the *Paydretz* adore Charette is perhaps that they have found in him a general in their own image ...

We can also understand how absence of consensus makes repression more difficult and can in fact prolong the rebellion. Whereas the massive uprising in the Pays des Mauges collapses completely by the end of 1793, here the rebels hold out until 1796.

*The beguiling Madame Bulkeley, née Talour de la Cartrie, one of Charette's proudest amazons, does not merely shine at the Court at Legé. She also leads a squad of cavalry, and receives two sabre wounds at Torfou. Captured together with her husband, she escapes execution by claiming to be pregnant, then loses no time in taking up arms once more at Charette's side. Indefatigable in marriage, she remarries for the fourth time in 1804.*

By late June 1793, the revolt is already experiencing grave setbacks, which are unfailingly blamed on Charette, as impetuous and independent as ever.

## "My *Paydretz* shall take Luçon all on their own"

In the beginning, his relations with the other generals are excellent. Lescure congratulates Charette on the capture of Machecoul and proposes that he invest Nantes from the south on 29th June, while the Grand Army attacks via the right bank of the

**THE GRAND ARMY IS CRUSHED**

Loire. Charette opens fire at two o'clock in the morning, whereas the others experience their first major failure, in the face of heroic republican resistance.

The defeat at Luçon, on 14th August, has absolutely disasterous effects. On the day before the battle, the other generals, who bring with them over forty thousand men, speak ironically of Charette's seven thousand *Paydretz*. The latter, in his annoyance, replies that they shall take Luçon all on their own. On the following day they attack too early, while the Grand Army is immobilized by its commanders' disagreements. Five thousand Vendéens meet their deaths on the plain. "Never shall it be said that I abandoned any of my men", exclaims Charette in the midst of the rout, loading a wounded soldier onto his own horse. Stuck together by the man's dried blood, general and soldier will only be pulled apart with difficulty : a most eloquent symbol.

## Charette again goes it alone

The rebellion's days are now numbered, since the Republicans have dispatched the famous soldiers of the Mainz battalions, commanded by Kléber, to put down the insurrection. Anxious to cut off all seaborne aid to the rebels, the republican forces begin their offensive in Charette's sector. Fleeing their burning villages and hindered by the presence of non-combatants, the *Paydretz* fall back on the Grand Army. At Torfou, their womenfolk have to take up the cudgels to force the Vendéens to resume the fight. By the evening, for all their belittling comments about "Mainz mice", the Vendéens' victory only gives momentary respite. For failing to follow up his advantage by pursuing another troop then burning Saint-Fulgent, Charette is accused of losing the Vendéens the opportunity to finish off the Mainz battalions. He now goes it alone, for good.

## The guerrilla war starts

Defeated at Cholet on 17th October, the Grand Army crosses the Loire in poor shape. Now cut off from their own land and lifeline, these Vendéens see their tragic combat ended at Savenay on 26th December, in a bloodbath. Meanwhile Charette has retaken the island of Noirmoutier, on 12th October. By early November, Haxo's Republicans believe their enemy surrounded at Bouin. Just after daybreak, they attack the village itself : there is no trace of Charette. From now on, Charette will only fight on his own terms. He has started his guerrilla war.

*A soldier of the Mainz battalions.*

31

And yet by early 1794, the War of the Vendée appears to be over. On 3rd January, Haxo and Jordy accept the surrender of Noirmoutier's defenders. Seeing matters differently, the representatives of the people order the execution of some twelve hundred persons, including Commanding General d'Elbée, previously wounded at Cholet, who is shot while still seated in his chair.

# THE LION BECOMES A FOX

*Too weak to stand, d'Elbée has to be carried in his chair before the firing squad. (Julien le Blant, 1878).*

For his part, Charette has hastened inland, where he attempts to regroup the fragments of the Vendéen army. For La Rochejaquelein, the Grand Army Commander who has managed to recross the Loire, all Charette deigns to offer is a place on his own staff. These questions of rank are preposterous : the young Commander is killed shortly afterwards, and in any case none left wants to fight on.

## The infernal columns rekindle the flames

*The story goes that, following the execution of the four ladies of La Métairie, all cousins of Charette, and of their maidservant, the executioner returned home in a fit of delirium, and died three days later.*

General Turreau now unleashes his infernal columns on the Vendée. By declaration of the Convention, "It is necessary for the Vendée to be annihilated, for daring to doubt the benefits of Liberty." Because victory is not enough, the Republicans embark upon the destruction of an entire region and the deliberate slaughter of its population. If, as horror-stricken witnesses to the barbarous treatment of women and children, the Vendeéns themselves appear to suffer from amnesia, numerous accounts do survive. Though hard to believe, they are provided by the Republicans themselves. Will we ever know even the number of victims ? No other region paid such a heavy tribute to the Terror.

All over the region, this gratuitous savagery only serves to bring Charette new recruits and triggers a second revolt, which is all the more terrible as it is born of despair.

*"What a great pity it is that such a decent man should be killed,"* exclaims Charette, distressed to hear of Haxo's death, on 20th March 1794. Fiercely opposed to Turreau's orders, this white-haired giant of a man had even refused to burn down Fonteclose, Charette's residence.

## The elusive enemy

This ex-serviceman must now leave behind all notions of regiments on the march or towns captured and defended. A distant precursor of Giap and Mao, Charette founds his strategy on complete mobility. "It is no easy thing to track down Charette, and still less so to do battle with him," attests Haxo. "One day he heads ten thousand men, the next day he roves with twenty soldiers at most. You believe him before you, he is behind your columns : he threatens a certain position, then he is ten leagues away soon after. Skilled at eluding battle, he seeks only to surprise you, to put your patrols and scouts to the sword and to seize your convoys." One month later, this valorous Republican falls at Les Clouzeaux.

## States of deadlock

Both sides are now ensnared in their own contradictions. Rather than accept Charette as their leader, the Royalists prefer an ineffectual collective leadership. As Marigny soon breaks his promises, the others sentence him to death. The seeds of discord soon burgeon with Stofflet as well.

*Turreau, the man behind the infernal columns.*

On the republican side, Turreau's loathsome plan, now proved to be absurd, is abandoned and fortified camps established instead, to little avail. It would be as well to acknowledge that the military approach has failed. The only answer is a political solution, which must await the fall of Robespierre.

In checking the wave of terrorism which had fomented the revolt, the 9th Thermidor* revolutionaries deprive the rebellion of its lifeblood. A deep weariness has taken hold of the combatants, against which the hardliners struggle in vain. And now, in the impending peace negotiations, too long isolated to measure the far-reaching impact of revolutionary ideas, the Vendéens will reveal their own naïvety in the face of the astuteness displayed anew by the republican diplomatists.

# LONG LIVE CHARETTE ! SHOUT THE REPUBLICANS

## The Vendéen General, the beautiful Creole and the representative of the people

"Please forgive me, this is all I have left," smiles Madame Gasnier as she sets out cups for her republican guests on a tablecloth embroidered with royal fleurs-de-lis. Why cannot representatives of the people still maintain their republican principles <u>and</u> enjoy the coffee served by this captivating Creole with her *Ancien Régime* charms ? Representative Ruelle looks lasciviously upon Madame Gasnier's maidservant. He reflects on the order which he has received to have done with the Vendéen question, but is as yet unaware that this maidservant is none other than Charette's own sister, who from her refuge in Nantes warns the Vendéens of the Republicans' movements.

*The La Jaunaie peace treaty, as shown by Girardet.*

* date of the coup which brought down Robespierre.

*Charette's triumphal entry into Nantes.*

## Secret clauses ?

Helped on by the coffee, contact is soon established. The first talks are held on 12th February 1795, in a tent near the Château de la Jaunaie, not far from Nantes. More elegant than ever, Charette sports a hat decorated with coloured plumes : white for royalty, black for mourning, green for hope. But no matter : only too happy to have survived the Terror, they rediscover life's culinary pleasures while evoking past battles.

Hard negotiations end in a peace treaty being signed on 17th February. Since then, the existence of secret clauses providing for the restoration of the monarchy has often been suggested. What is the outcome ? The Republicans have given ground on almost all points : the Vendéens will be exempt from military service and war veterans living locally will be employed to maintain the rule of law. All will be indemnified ; the question of taxes will be settled later. There will be freedom of worship. While as regards the form of régime, the representatives argue that the time is not yet ripe for the King's return to be envisaged.

## A fool's bargain

Backed by the verbal promises made, perhaps to the effect that Louis XVII, the prisoner in the Temple, would be delivered to him, Charette compels silence from his detractors. In fact, the treaty amounts to a *de facto* recognition of the Republic. The ebbing tide of revolutionary opinion acknowledges the legitimacy of the motives behind the rebellion.

Although not all the hatreds engendered can be erased, this development does create an irresistible dynamic current for peace.

The sight is quite remarkable : republican blue and royalist white join together in a procession before the people of Nantes, who, on 26th February, acclaim the Convention, Charette and above all the new-found peace. This time, the Vendéen General has to swap his white panache for plumes in the national colours ...

The next time he sees Nantes, it will be for his execution.

*"Here is the place to strike a man of courage," Charette is reputed to have said, pointing to his chest. (Julien le Blant 1883).*

*"My dear Dumouriez, kindly tell the son of Citizen Equality to go to hell."*

Charette, on 21st November 1795, to Dumouriez, who offered him the chance to hand the crown to the son of Philippe-Égalité, the regicidal cousin of Louis XVI.

Charette has taken all these initiatives under the pressure of immediate necessity. And now, having previously remained strangely silent, the Princes at last realize the Vendée's importance.

## "The second founder of the monarchy"

On 1st February 1795, from Verona, the Regent proclaims his admiration for Charette. He calls him nothing less than "the second founder of the monarchy" and expresses his fervent desire to come to the Vendée and share in his perils and his glory. One can imagine Charette's disquiet

## "TELL THE PRINCE THAT HE PASSES SENTENCE OF DEATH UPON ME "

on receiving such a consecration, when he has just signed the La Jaunaie treaty. "If I examine my inner self," he says in self-justification, "I find deep in my heart the indelible honour of the true French knight." It follows that the peace proves increasingly flimsy. When the prisoner in the Temple dies on 8th June, the Royalists see in this the work of poison.

On the 25th, the day before the émigrés land at Quiberon, Charette re-opens hostilities by capturing the republican camp at Les Essarts. On 8th July, the Regent appoints him Commander-in-Chief. "I hereby renew my forever inviolable vow," he proclaims on the 23rd, at his headquarters at Belleville, "only to lay down my arms once the heir apparent is on the throne of France." He calls above all for a prince of the blood to come to the Vendée, to restore the inhabitants' morale and efface their divisions.

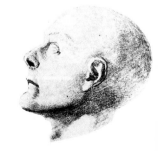

## A now hopeless sense of loyalty

Because neither the heart, nor perhaps the soul, is in it anymore. From offering resistance to oppression, the Royalists are now in the service of a cause. When, on 9th August, Charette learns that the Quiberon émigrés have been slaughtered following their surrender, he returns barbarity for barbarity and has three hundred prisoners executed.

On 16th September, he at last receives a letter from the Regent's brother, the Count d'Artois, who announces that he is to land with fifteen hundred troops. Yet none arrive on the appointed date. "Tell the Prince that he passes sentence of death upon me," declares Charette to his emissary. "Today, I have fifteen thousand men about me ; tomorrow, I will not even have three hundred left. My only course is to go into hiding or to die fighting : I choose to die."

In response to the Republicans who offer him a safe-conduct, to the clerics who forsake him, or to his officers who advise him to abandon the fight, Charette's only answer lies in loyalty : which although now hopeless, does not lack panache. On 28th February, he enjoins his partisans to abandon him. He will pay the price in the woods at La Chabotterie.

On 29th March 1796, at the Place des Agriculteurs in Nantes, Charette stands alone before the firing squad. He refuses to be blindfolded and insists that he himself be allowed to give the order to fire. After the volley of shots, the body remains upright for a moment, like the man who, until the very end and even in its very contradictions, continued to embody the Vendée.

*Citizen Casanne, a plasterer, was allowed to make a cast of Charette's face, in the quarry at Gigant, where his corpse had been dumped. It is there, somewhere beside the Rennes road, that Charette's mortal remains lie to this day, along with those of so many other victims.*

39

# IN THE FOOTSTEPS OF CHARETTE

Leaving behind La Chabotterie and its evocations of Charette to hunt for the hero's shade, visitors run the risk of bitter disappointment : the landscapes have changed, the monuments themselves have often been subject to alteration and naturally, the Vendéens of today are not their distant forebears.

Need the search be abandoned, however, and history lived only through books ? I think not : those willing to spend the time can still discover beside a sunken lane a hedgerow which Charette may have crossed, or the building which once gave him shelter and now willingly reveals its secrets to those possessing imagination, or perhaps above all the Vendéens themselves, who as in times past are inaccessible to those who treat them with disdain or seek to hem them in, but remain deeply attached to their roots and friendly towards those who go part of the way with them.

Let us trust such encounters to chance or to providence, to evoke the places which still bear witness to this tragically brief adventure.

*An official portrait of Charette, produced in 1819 by Paul Guérin, at the request of Louis XVIII.*

*An old photograph of Belleville.*

# A SIMPLE KNIGHT CALLED CHARETTE

Charette is born on 21st April 1763, at Couffé near Ancenis, at the manor-house of La Contrie, or perhaps in a house close to the church.

Near La Garnache, on the edge of the Breton marshlands, a tiled rooftop emerges from a maze of bocage hedgerows : Fonteclose, a Vendéen manor-house touching in its simplicity, with a rustic kitchen garden adjoining and vague defensive work in front. Charette was attempting to keep himself out of the way here when, on 14th March, having risen in revolt four days previously, the peasant folk called on him to become their leader.

Together with La Chabotterie, Fonteclose remains the principal monument to be properly identified with Charette's memory. On 4th September 1938, the Baudry d'Asson family, the house's owners since 1860, made Fonteclose the setting for a commemoration presenting the main episodes in Charette's life, enacted by two hundred and forty volunteers before no less than twenty-five thousand spectators.

*The Breton marshland in winter.*

*The old Fonteclose.*

*The manor-house of La Contrie, the church at Couffé and the entrance to the village.*

# THE START OF THE REVOLT IN THE PAYS DE RETZ AREA

As the main scene of revolt in the Pays de Retz area, Machecoul was soon presented in revolutionary propaganda as the principal breeding ground for the rebels' bloody fanaticism. A dark legend which served as the pretext for savage, meaningless acts of repression.

In capturing the small seaport of Pornic, Charette gives his troops their first victory on 27th March.

*The old Château overlooking the Port of Noirmoutier.*

# NOIRMOUTIER, KEY TO THE ATLANTIC OCEAN

Unused up until 1770, at the time of the War of the Vendée the Passage du Gois causeway is still a dangerous passage barely exposed at low tide. Yet the different antagonists choose to invest the island of Noirmoutier by this route, and sometimes also by sea.

Noirmoutier offered the rebels a means of access to foreign aid. Captured by the Vendéens on 16th March 1793, the island is retaken by Beysser on 29th April, then by Charette in the night of 11th to 12th October. On the 21st, the Executive Revolutionary Council orders "the island to be retaken or engulfed by the sea". On 3rd January 1794, Noirmoutier falls into republican hands. The representatives of the people have twelve to fifteen hundred of the island's defenders massacred, despite their capitulation. Commanding General d'Elbée, who had taken refuge on Noirmoutier after being wounded at Cholet, is shot while still seated in his chair, being too weak to stand.

*The causeway known as Le Gois.*

*"Ever faithful to God and King, Charette was only ever unfaithful to his mistresses."*

Le Bouvier-Desmortiers, his first biographer, in 1809.

## THE COURT AT LEGÉ

The view from Legé takes in most of what was once Charette's territory. This hilltop is where he most logically chooses to set up his headquarters from May to September 1793, ordering ditches to be dug and trees felled in the vicinity. Here, between two expeditions, war is forgotten amid dancing and lovemaking, at the court where the very beautiful Madame de la Rochefoucauld reigns supreme. In the street which goes by this name, near the church, a small house bearing the inscription *Deus spes nostra* 1663 is supposed to have accommodated Charette.

A short respite indeed, before the outburst of fury by the republican troops billeted at Legé, who in early 1794 are responsible for massacring the inhabitants of the surrounding districts. "The corpses of women and children, laid out in all the villages with a barbaric symmetry of which savages would not have been capable," reports a reliable witness, "appeared to demand vengeance from the kinsmen who survived them."

In remembrance, the Chapel of Notre-Dame de Pitié, otherwise known as Charette's Chapel, was built under the Restoration, in 1825-1826. On the day of its inauguration by two bishops and eighty priests, three thousand former companions-in-arms of the King of Legé are passed in review. But in 1832, soldiers sent by the Orleanist Government to hunt for the Duchess de Berry, who is in hiding in the district, wreck the sanctuary and destroy Charette's statue.

*"Deus spes nost[ra]*
*- in God our ho[pe]*
*the inscription above [the]*
*door to the house in wh[ich]*
*Charette is supposed to h[ave]*
*stayed at Le[gé]*

*Legé dominates the surrounding bocage landscape.*

*The chapel at Legé and the monument to Charette, around 1830 ...*

*... and today.*

# THE MARTYRDOM OF LES LUCS

*The agony of Father Voyneau, as depicted in a stained-glass window in the church at Les Lucs.*

The small town of Les Lucs is sometimes known as the Vendéen Oradour*, since on 28th February 1794 General Cordellier's columns, then pursuing Charette, slaughter a large number of the inhabitants of Le Grand-Luc, then on 5th March proceed to massacre the parishioners who had sought refuge in the church at Le Petit-Luc. According to the list drawn up shortly after these events by the parish priest, Father Barbedette, no less than five hundred and sixty-four persons, including one hundred and ten children under seven years of age, met their deaths in this way. The infernal columns certainly did not only wreak their terror at Les Lucs, and there as elsewhere such acts of barbarity leave the survivors as if stricken with amnesia. But even allowing for possible mistakes, this macabre body count closely reflects the terrible reality and goes to explain the importance ascribed by the Vendéens to the martyrology compiled by Father Barbedette.

*\* Oradour-sur-Glane, scene of a similar massacre by the Nazis in June 1944.*

*The interminable list of victims on the walls of the chapel at Les Lucs.*

*The chapel at Les Lucs, a leading memorial to the victims of the War of the Vendée.*

```
        LA BROMIERE
JEAN MARTIN                 72 A
SON FILS FRANÇOIS           27 A
M.A.BOUHAUD NÉE MARTIN 36 A
CNE JOLY NÉE MARTIN         36 A
SA FILLE MARIE ANNE          2 A
JEAN SORIN                  28 A
SON EP MARIE MARTIN         30 A
LEURS 2 ENF JEAN & JUES4 A&  5 M
MATHURIN MALIDIN            28 A
G.RICOULEAU MALIDIN         52 A
```

```
JOSEPH PEYRE                40 A
SON EP JOUETTE BOURON       36 A
LEURS 3 FILLES MARIE ANNE 11 A
ANNE & JEANNE             9 & 5 A
M RENAUDIN GAUTHIER         72 A
M GIRARD NÉE JARNY          57 A
SES 3 ENF PIERRE             6 A
MARIE JEANNE & JEAN 4&       1 A
LOUIS TENET                 66 A
SON EP LOUISE REMAUD        46 A
LEURS 3 FILLES JEANNE       14 A
MARIE MADELEINE             10 A
```

```
MARIE GARREAU               47 A
JEAN GIRAUDET               26 A
FRANÇOIS SAVARIAU           55 A
SON FILS FRANÇOIS           54 A
M VRIGNAUD V VRIGNAUD 84 A
JEAN VRIGNAUD               60 A
JEAN SON FILS               50 A
SES 2 ENF JEAN BAPTISTE      4 A
ET MARIE JEANNE              3 A
        LA DEVINIERE
TH CHARRIER GRASSET         70 A
```

# GRASLA, OR EVERYDAY LIFE AT THE TIME OF THE INFERNAL COLUMNS

On 22nd February, the butchers descend on Les Brouzils, and the following day on Chavagnes-en-Paillers. One can understand why the nearby forest of Grasla, which sometimes shelters Charette, soon attracts increasing numbers of refugees from the surrounding areas. Shielded by dense thickets, where the infernal columns hesitate to penetrate, the forest clearings soon accommodate some two thousand persons. And, in their turfed lodgings, it could almost be said that life resumed its normal course : makeshift mills are constructed for grinding corn, and children are even baptized.

Without any sense of bitterness or obsession with the past, nine neighbouring districts have joined together to recreate this astonishing testimony to their history and to welcome visitors to this site.

*After the fight.*
*(Evariste Carpentier, 1883).*

# AT HIS BELLEVILLE HEADQUARTERS, CHARETTE AWAITS LOUIS XVII

From the spring of 1794 to the winter of 1795, Charette makes his capital at Belleville, which has been spared by the infernal columns. In the absence of sufficiently accurate accounts, all the historian has to go on is tradition, which designates the Domaine de la Jarriette as his *headquarters*, one building as the *officers' mess* and another as the *royal palace*.

The royal prisoner in the Temple dies on 8th June 1795. At Belleville, on 23rd July, Charette vows not to lay down his arms until the monarchy is restored.

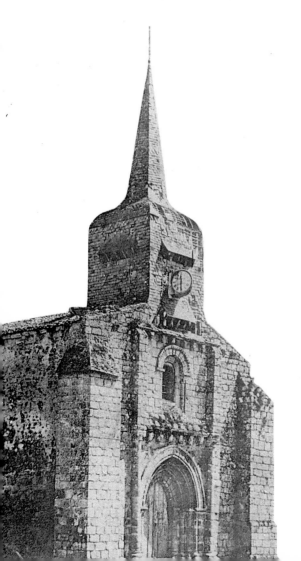

*The old church, dating from the late XIIth century, and its porch, the only feature to have been spared by the zeal of catholicism, which is triumphant here in the late XIXth century (1875) and more concerned with building edifices to its own tastes than preserving medieval monuments. While his chaplain, Father Remaud, was celebrating mass, Charette is supposed to have had prisoners executed in retaliation for the massacre at Quiberon.*

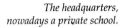
The headquarters,
nowadays a private school.

The street of
the officers' mess.

The building known as
the royal palace, despite
the fact that the date
1836 is inscribed on the
lintel. This residence
was reportedly built by
Charette to
accommodate Louis

XVII, whom the
republican negotiators at
La Jaunaie had promised
to hand over to him. Even
if this is a legend, does
this tradition not have
historical significance in
itself ?

# CHARETTE AND NANTES

## The besieger

On 29th June 1793, from the Loire's south bank, Charette and around ten thousand men attempt to counter the perpetual threat posed to the Vendéens by the City of Nantes. The failure of the attack and Cathelineau's death represent the first major setback for the revolt.

## The peacemaker

Charette makes an almost triumphal entry into Nantes on 27th February 1795, following the signing of the La Jaunaie peace treaty. In front of Bouffay Prison, in a gesture soon copied by the Republicans, he removes his hat and stands in long salute to this symbol of the Terror.

## The vanquished

Wounded at La Chabotterie, incarcerated at Bouffay Prison, paraded through the streets by hardhearted victors, Charette is shot on 29th March 1796, on the present-day Place Viarme.

*The attack on Nantes by the Vendéens (Désiré Lacroix).*

The Château de la Jaunaie.

Bouffay Prison, as
depicted by Tom Drake.

| CHARETTE | | THE CONTEXT |
|---|---|---|
| François-Athanase Charette de la Contrie is born at Couffé, near Ancenis. | **21st April 1763** | |
| He joins the navy and takes part in the American War. | **1779** | |
| | **1789** | The Revolution causes France's old monarchical régime to collapse. |
| Charette retires to the manor-house of Fonteclose. | **1790** | |
| | **1791-1792** | |

*The installation of the new régime creates growing discontent among the future Vendéen rebels.*

| | **10th August 1792** | |
|---|---|---|

*Now returned from exile, Charette joins in the defence of the Tuileries, against the attempts of the people of Paris to apprehend the King.*

| | **21st January 1793** | Execution of Louis XVI. |
|---|---|---|
| Six thousand peasants invade Machecoul on 11th March, slaughtering twenty or more national guards who had opened fire. On the 14th, they persuade Charette to leave his manor-house and become their leader. On the 27th, he gives them their first victory with the capture of Pornic. | **March 1793** | Refusing to be sent to the frontiers to defend a Republic which offends their religious convictions, the Vendéens rise in revolt. The Convention decrees that all rebels shall be put to death. |
| With difficulty, Charette succeeds ine defying both his rivals and incursions by Republicans from Les Sables and Nantes. | **April/May/ June 1793** | The Grand Royalist and Catholic Army captures Cholét, Bressuire, Thouars, Fontenay, Saumur and Angers. |
| | **29th June 1793** | |

*While Charette's troops besiege Nantes from the south without success, the Grand Army commanded by Cathelineau fails in its attack from the right bank.*

| | **1st août 1793** | The Convention decides on the complete destruction of the Vendée. |
|---|---|---|

*Not a sail on the horizon. The Count d'Artois will r*
*no hope. So much so that he la*